Primary Questions and Prompts

Margaret Jeffcoat
Margaret Jones
Jill Mansergh
John Mason
Heather Sewell
Anne Watson

Adapted from
Questions and Prompts
for Mathematical Thinking
by Anne Watson & John Mason
published by ATM in 1998.

ATM
Association of Teachers of Mathematics

Published in March 2004 by ATM

ATM would like to thank Barwell Infant School, Leicestershire and Gaddesby Primary School, Leicestershire for their contribution to this book.

Association of Teachers of Mathematics

7, Shaftesbury Street, Derby DE23 8YB

Telephone: 01332 346599

Fax: 01332 204357

e-mail: admin@atm.org.uk

Copyright © 2004
Margaret Jeffcoat, Margaret Jones, Jill Mansergh
John Mason, Heather Sewell, Anne Watson

All trademarks are the property of their respective owners

All rights reserved

Printed in England

ISBN 1 898611 27 0

Copies may be purchased from the above address or http://www.atm.org.uk

FOREWORD

The questions and prompts in this book arise from considering some of the work of Zygfryd Dyrszlag, a Polish mathematics educator. He produced a list of 63 questions which teachers can ask pupils in order both to promote, and to monitor the development of pupils' concepts. His list was translated for us by Anna Sierpinska. The questions resonated with our sense of mathematical thinking and mathematical structure, and stimulated us to identify some themes and structure underlying the questions so that we could integrate the wealth of ideas into a useful collection for ourselves and perhaps colleagues. Our development of the questions may bear no relationship to Dyrszlag's intentions; what follows is therefore an example of how chance encounters with ideas can, with thought and discussion, trial and reflection, trigger changes of practice.

CONTENTS

1 Introduction 6

2 Questioning and Prompting
   Ways of Talking About Mathematics in Classrooms 7
   Questioning 7

3 A View of Mathematics
   Structures in Mathematics 9
   Mathematical Thinking 9

4 General Questions and Prompts 10

5 How questions and prompts might be used
   Example 1: planning to teach fractions using questions and prompts ... 12
   Example 2: exploring boundaries 13

6 Specific Questions 15
   Exemplifying, Specialising 16/17
   Completing, Deleting, Correcting 18/19
   Comparing, Sorting, Organising 20/21
   Changing, Varying, Reversing, Altering 22/23
   Generalising, Conjecturing 24/25
   Explaining, Justifying, Verifying, Refuting 26/27

7 Dryrszlag's Original List 28

8 Background
   Questioning as Social and Psychological Activity 29
   Questioning in Different Ways 29
   Questioning Ourselves 30
   Questioning Questioning 30
   Questioning for Learning Mathematics 31
   Questioning Understanding 31
   Questioning Which Reflects Mathematical Structure 32
   Belief About Teaching 32

Bibliography 33

Blank Grid 35

1 - INTRODUCTION

Questions such as

How did you ...?, Why does ...?, and What if ...?

are typical questions intended to provoke children into becoming aware of mathematical thinking processes, into encountering convincing and proving, and into exploration. When we ask these questions we expect to focus children's thinking on structures and processes of mathematical thinking, but in fact they often find such questions difficult to address. We have found that questions like:

**Give me an example of...,
Is it always, sometimes, or never true that...?
What more can be imposed on this and it still be an example of ...?**

reflect more closely both mathematical structure and ways of mathematical thinking. The struggle to express ideas is an important part of learning. It is easier for children who are talking about their own ideas to understand that expressions can be more precise with the use of technical terms.

This booklet sets out some questions which can be asked about mathematical topics. They reflect internal structures of mathematics and mathematical thinking, as we see them. They can therefore be used for:

- whole class teaching;
- individual teaching;
- private study;
- planning to teach a topic;
- revising a topic;
- monitoring understanding.

The questions are certainly not a recipe for teaching mathematics, nor even a menu from which one can choose. Rather they are intended as a source of inspiration and as an aid to change. The grid of questions we have produced is a '*net to catch the practice of effective mathematicians*', as one participant in a workshop described it.

2 - QUESTIONING and PROMPTING

As teachers we tend to use both questions and prompts to try to provoke pupils into thinking, to try to focus their attention. We use prompt to refer to statements like "**Tell me ..**" which are essentially questions in that they expect a pupil response, even if there is no question mark, no raising of voice tones at the end.

Ways of talking in classrooms about mathematics

The questions and prompts we offer are based on our knowledge of mathematics and how we and others teach it and learn it. Our interest is in using mathematical questions as prompts and devices for promoting pupils in thinking mathematically, and thus becoming better at learning and doing mathematics. Although we devised many of the questions from a theoretical base, we often found ourselves remarking "*this is what I do*" or "*this is what X or Y does*". We have seen a variety of questions used in many classrooms in the UK, and in other countries, which are clearly directed towards the development of mathematical thinking. On the other hand, we have also seen lessons and textbooks in which a very limited range of questions and prompts are used, geared mainly towards expressing particular techniques, finding answers or checking correct use of technical terms. We have also seen lessons and textbooks in which mathematical thinking is only made explicit in content-free investigative work, or in practical tasks. The suggested approaches are usually low-level applications of problem-solving techniques, such as trial-and-adjustment or creating formulae from tables of values. We hope our work will show how *higher order mathematical thinking* can be provoked and promoted as an integral part of teaching and learning core school mathematics, through the teacher's leadership and example.

The teacher and/or text provide the pupils with a model of how mathematics can be questioned and discussed. The nature and range of questions and prompts used by the teacher, either in whole class interactive sessions or in one-to-one and small group interactions, can affect how mathematics is seen and discussed in all interactions in the classroom, however they are initiated and whomever they are between.

A balance has to be struck between using a limited range of questions, leading to boredom and a narrow view of mathematical thinking, and a confusing variety of approaches. The aim should be to offer a range of questions, interesting enough to maintain attention, repeated often enough, and with enough similarity, for the pupil to become familiar with their style. Hence pupils can be encouraged to take over the responsibility for asking questions themselves. An ultimate aim would be that pupils could use such approaches in discussions with each other.

The questions collected in this booklet provide a huge range of possibilities, not only for classroom discussion on every level, but also as starters for mathematical tasks. However, they are not a method in themselves, nor are they intended to provide the only form of interaction or the only teaching. A lesson built around these questions alone would neither give time for practice, nor for closely-focused work on individual problems and needs.

Questioning

It is common to think about questions as being either open or closed. For example,

> **"What is 3 + 4?"**

is usually seen as closed because there is a definite answer, and

> **"What pairs of numbers can be added to give 7"**

is by contrast usually seen as open because there are many possible answers. In both cases the person asking the questions has criteria for what is an acceptable response, and it may even be that the intention of the 'open' questions is to focus on expressing the generality of all possible answers. Thus most 'closed' questions can be opened up, and many apparently 'open' questions are nevertheless constrained.

We find it necessary to go beyond this simple categorisation and ask questions which, whether interpreted as open or closed, promote thought about the structure of a concept. Such questions depend not on recall, but on pupils' willingness to participate in a collective struggle for understanding. Answers are unlikely to be wrong in a traditional sense, because they are genuine responses to genuine enquiry, rather than a form of testing. A sensitive teacher will listen to answers and think: "*what does that response reveal about understanding?*" and adjust the lesson accordingly.

Many of the prompts we offer are invitations to pupils to do something, say something or suggest something. In some cases only one answer will be appropriate, while in others many responses might legitimately be made. The possible range of answers might depend on the current state of knowledge of the pupil, or the whole class. Openness and closure of questions are therefore relative to the teaching context.

Beginning teachers and others are often reluctant to generate discussion in the classroom because they may be worried about whether they will be able to deal with unexpected responses. They may prefer to stick with questions to which they already know the answers. Certainly it can be unsettling when pupils' responses are unexpected, but usually such situations are stimulating and revealing. As long as teachers see themselves as enquirers struggling for comprehension of the pupils' thinking, then the worst that can happen is that unexpected responses are recorded as conjectures or issues for further consideration.

3 - A VIEW OF MATHEMATICS

Our view of mathematics draws upon our experience with 'structures' of pure mathematics and with 'processes' of mathematical thinking. The questions arise from applying different processes to different structures.

Structures in Mathematics

Within any mathematics topic there are a variety of forms of mathematical statements which can be made. Some are quite distinctive; others differ only in subtle ways.

List A: Mathematical Statements

- Definitions
- Counterexamples
- Representations
- Links
- Facts
- Techniques
- Notation
- Relationships
- Theorems
- Instructions
- Explanations
- Connections
- Properties
- Conjectures
- Justifications
- Examples
- Problems
- Reasoning

The collection of statements of different types which make up a topic provides the structure for that topic. Thus we see each teacher and each pupil as having their own structure for each topic, according to which types of statements they stress and in which ways they see connections between them.

Once we are aware of how many different aspects there might be to a topic we are free to choose to start *wherever we like*. Our choices will inevitably be related to how we see the topic and how we think our pupils will learn it best, but stating the list in this form might also prompt us to consider other ways of starting. It is important to introduce children to ways of mathematical thinking. Indeed, this may almost be more important than the mathematical topics taught! Freshness can be kept by varying the use of different prompts.

For example, you could start by offering the class a *problem*, and then after an initial period of thinking, engage the class in discussing possible *techniques*, useful *facts* and *reasoning*, before allowing individuals or groups to choose a promising way to work on it. You could also work through an *example* publicly, or work through an example by considering *conjectures*, or taking *instructions* from the class about *techniques*. You could also begin by raising issues from previous topics, or even other subjects, and generate new questions which direct attention to the current topic, thus displaying *links* and *connections*.

Mathematical Thinking

There are various kinds of mental activity which, together, typify mathematical thinking:

List B: Mathematical Activities

- exemplifying
- comparing
- reversing
- justifying
- specialising
- sorting
- altering
- verifying
- completing
- organising
- generalising
- refuting
- deleting
- changing
- conjecturing
- correcting
- varying
- explaining

We have deliberately omitted more obvious activities which take place in mathematics lesson such as calculating, solving, drawing, plotting, graphing and measuring because we are only interested in the subset of the activities of mathematics which are associated with thinking, reasoning and coming to know a concept, rather than with rehearsing in order to produce correct and fluent performance, or to generate data and raw material for mathematics.

4 - GENERAL QUESTIONS AND PROMPTS

By considering activities in list B, grouped under six collective headings for convenience, we developed several general questions and prompts which can be used by while teaching. Some of these arose from recalling our own practice or from watching other teachers, and some came from Dyrszlag (see Foreword and Section 7). Others arose from considering how we might use these activities in particular mathematical contexts, or from discussions with others.

Exemplifying Specialising	Completing Deleting Correcting	Comparing Sorting Organising	Changing Varying Reversing Altering	Generalising Conjecturing	Explaining Justifying Verifying Refuting

List B grouped

Under each heading we generated appropriate generic questions.

Exemplifying Specialising	Completing Deleting Correcting	Comparing Sorting Organising
Give me one or more examples of… Describe, Demonstrate, Tell, Show, Choose, Draw, Find, Locate, an example of… Is… an example of…? What makes… an example? Find a counter-example of…	What <u>must</u> be added, removed, altered, in order to allow, ensure, contradict,…? What <u>can</u> be added, removed, altered, without affecting …? Tell me what is wrong with …. What needs to be changed so that…?	What is the same and different about…? Sort or organise the following according to… Is it or is it not…?

Changing Varying Reversing Altering	Generalising Conjecturing	Explaining Justifying Verifying Refuting
What do you get if you change…? What if…? If this is the answer to a similar question, what was the question? Do… in two (or more) ways. What is quickest, easiest,…?	Of what is this an example? What happens in general? Is it always, sometimes, never …? Describe all possible… as succinctly as you can. What can change and what has to stay the same so that… is still true?	Explain why…, Give a reason… How can we be sure that…? Tell me what is wrong with… Is it always true that…? How is… used in…? Explain role or use of…

We then applied these general questions to List A, grouped under eight collective headings, to produce the grid on the next page. A full page copy of this grid can be found on the last page of the booklet.

	Exemplifying Specialising	Completing Deleting Correcting	Comparing Sorting Organising	Changing Varying Reversing Altering	Generalising Conjecturing	Explaining Justifying Verifying Refuting
Vocabulary and Definitions						
Facts, Theorems and Properties						
Examples and Counter-examples						
Techniques and Instructions						
Conjectures and Problems						
Representations and Notation						
Explanations Justifications Reasoning						
Links Relationships Connections						

There is no mechanical procedure used to produce questions to fill this grid. Inspired by Dyrszlag's questions, we generated them from our sense of mathematics, and our intention is that they point to aspects of mathematical thinking. They are intended to prompt or provoke similar questions in you, not act as fixed and rigid questions. We find they work best for us when they are used flexibly to structure our preparation and when they inform our choice of question to ask within a framework of key questions for a lesson. When they become rigid and mechanical they lose their power.

Even the selected questions listed on the previous page make a daunting collection, and many may be obscure at the moment. It is not a matter of 'learning' all the questions, but rather of developing one's own sense of mathematics so that these questions and variants of them come to mind in the midst of interactions with pupils. Over time this will happen, but to start with, we recommend taking one question type and making explicit use of it whenever possible, in order to get a sense of what it generates. It is very likely that if one or two particular questions as exemplified in the next section do not make much sense to you, then they may signal a fruitful area for investigation for you as mathematician, in order to extend your awareness of mathematical thinking in that direction.

Primary Questions & Prompts

5 - HOW QUESTIONS AND PROMPTS MIGHT BE USED

In working on questions for the grids we considered how this might relate to work in the classroom. We have prefaced the work on the grid with some examples of how it might be used. Reading these examples before you get to the grids may focus your thoughts as you read through the questions in the grid. The questions in the examples are organised sequentially starting with Year 1 through to Year 6, although many of the questions can be adapted for use in either key stage.

Our intention in providing these examples is to show how questions might be developed to help pupils learn, think and communicate mathematics.

Example 1: Planning to teach fractions using questions and prompts about fractions

In this example we used the grid on page 9 specifically to create new discussion points or starting points for the teaching of fractions. We thought about each cell of the grid with fractions in mind, asking ourselves, 'How can I ask this question about this kind of statement for this topic?' The important point was that the grid was an aid to creativity. A whole lesson might be created from one of the prompts, or by stringing several together. To use the prompts the teacher must have her own objectives based on what is appropriate for her class. We offer this as an illustration of how using the grid can lead you to think about old topics in new ways and generate discussion. The list is loosely ordered, but some of the questions can be adapted for the stage of development of the pupils. For example, find me 8/7 on a number line might read find me 1/2 on a number line or find me 3/10 on a number line.

1. Show me an example of a half – on a poster, on a shelf, on the table, on a page
2. Describe which features of 3/4 make it an example of a fraction greater than 1/2.
3. Show me how to change 1/2 into quarters
4. Find me 8/7 on a number line
5. Demonstrate 4/5 with a rectangle
6. Show 1/3 of 9 using a picture
7. Are there any fractions which are not less than 1?
8. How is halving used in dividing by 4?
9. Can you find other ways of writing these fractions so that they both have the same denominator?
10. What is the denominator? What is the numerator?
11. What is the same and what is different about 1/5 and 2/10?
12. Why does 1/2 of 1/2 give an answer which is less than 1/2?
13. Complete the missing parts in $\frac{42}{} = \frac{}{30} = 3.5$
14. What needs to be altered so that 0.3 = 1/3?
15. Fractions and decimals are the same in that . . . but different in that . . . .
16. Is 4/9 an example of a recurring decimal?
17. Put in order some instructions for converting fractions to decimals.
18. Put these in an order that makes it easy to convert from one to the next: fractions, percentages, decimals
19. Show 1/3 of 8 using a picture
20. If we eat 8 blocks of a bar of chocolate with 24 blocks we have eaten 1/3 of the bar. If we can see from the shape of the packet that we have eaten 1/3 of the bar can we say how many blocks we have eaten?
21. Tell me what is wrong with 1/2 + 1/2 = 2/4, 1/3 + 1/3 = 2/6

22. What is special about 3/16 add 13/16? Make up some more questions with this feature.

23. Sort these fractions from smallest to biggest.

24. What is the same and what is different about 2/3 and 9/5 as examples of fractions?

25. What is the same and what is different about 75% and 3/4?

26. If 1/3 is a recurring decimal is 2/3 a recurring decimal?

27. If 1/3 is a recurring decimal is 1/2 of 1/3 a recurring decimal?

Example 2: Exploring Boundaries

Here are some examples of sequences of challenges which are intended to provoke pupils to think more deeply about relationships within topics. The aim is to construct special examples which enable exploration of the concepts. The format was stimulated by the prompts to do with exemplifying, completing, deleting, comparing and generalising.

Whole Numbers

1. Write down a number
2. Write down a number that is smaller than 10
3. Write down a number that is smaller than 10 and bigger than 2.
4. Write down a number that is smaller than 10 and bigger than 2 and is an even number.

- Go back and make sure all your numbers are different.

- Are there any other possible answers you could have had for question 4?

Quadrilaterals

1. Draw a quadrilateral.
2. Draw a quadrilateral with one pair of opposite sides parallel.
3. Draw a quadrilateral with one pai r of opposite sides parallel and one pair of opposite angles equal.
4. Draw a quadrilateral with one pair of opposite sides parallel and one pair of opposite angles equal and diagonals intersecting at right angles.

- Now go back and make sure that each example gives a different quadrilateral.

- Are these the only examples?

- Can you make up a similar set of questions using triangles or other shapes?

Integers–division

1. Write down a number which leaves a remainder of 1 after division by 7.
2. Write down a number which leaves a remainder of 1 after division by 7 and is a perfect square.
3. Write down a number which leaves a remainder of 1 after division by 7 and is a perfect square and is a perfect cube.

- Now go back and make sure that each example gives a different integer.

- Are there any other answers?

- Can you construct a similar set of questions for division by another number, or leaving a different remainder?

Fractions

1. Write down an improper fraction.
2. Write down an improper fraction which lies between 3 and 4.
3. Write down an improper fraction which lies between 3 and 4 and is closer to 3 than 4.
4. Write down an improper fraction which lies between 3 and 4 and is closer to 3 than 4 and whose numerator differs from its denominator by a multiple of 3

- Make sure that each answer is a different improper fraction.

- If the question had suggested mixed number rather than improper fraction would the questions have needed to be phrased differently?

Decimals

1. Write down a number.
2. Write down a number lying between 7 and 8.
3. Write down a number lying between 7 and 8 which when you subtract the unit part and multiply by 10 lies between 1 and 2.
4. Write down a number lying between 7 and 8 which when you subtract the unit part and multiply by 10 lies between 1 and 2 and is closer to 2.

- Now go back and make sure each number is different.

- If the word number were to be replaced by 'two digit number' what changes could be made to the rest of the statements?

Other ways in which the grid might be used.

- The grid can help to plan the overall content of a sequence of lessons

- Use one or two cells of the grid to provoke specific questions about a particular topic

- The grid can be used to provide an interactive revision session

- The grid can be used to generate interesting approaches to standard topics

- Focus on one cell in the grid and generate questions that would fit across a range of topics in order to establish mathematical links between topics.

6 - SPECIFIC QUESTIONS

The following 12 pages contain examples of specific questions that teachers might ask while their pupils are working on some mathematics.

Each of the six activity headings in the table on page 11 are considered in turn.

For example, on pages 16 and 17 there are questions relating to Exemplifying and Specialising, grouped into the eight categories given in the rows of the table above.

The main questions appear in blue type, and there is room for you to add further examples of your own.

Vocabulary and Definitions

Show me an example of…
- a square in the classroom.
- a 2-digit number in the classroom.
- a fraction.
- a cuboid in the classroom.
- a 3D shape with two different-shaped faces.
- something which is longer/shorter and wider/narrower than this.
- something which is smaller but heavier than this.

- Pick out the hundredth part of 1.324.
- Draw an isosceles triangle which is also right-angled.

What is it about the one you chose which makes it an example of…?
- Describe what makes a triangle a triangle.
- Describe what makes a triangle an isosceles triangle.
- What is it about this object which makes it a cuboid?
- How do you know when something is a measure of length?

Facts, Theorems and Properties

Tell me something that must be true if…
- I add together two single digit numbers greater than 5.
- I add together two odd numbers.
- these three numbers are the angles of a triangle.

Tell me one (or more) properties…
- of the diagonals of a parallelogram.
- of a square in 15 seconds!
- that a fraction lying between 1 and 2 must have.

Describe the features of…
- a shape in a feely bag.
- a bar chart.
- a decimal (representation of) number.
- a parallelogram.

Examples and Counter-examples

Which features of… make it an example of…
- Which features of 32 show that it lies between 30 and 40?
- Which features of a number make it an example of a number which is easy to write in figures, but hard to say in words?
- Describe which features of 3/4 make it an example of a fraction greater than 1/2.
- Which features of a cuboid make it also a prism?
- Which features of a square make it a parallelogram?

Show me a counter-example to the claim that…
- for every positive integer there is a positive integer which is smaller than it.
- squaring a number makes it bigger.
- the larger the perimeter the larger the area.

Make up three questions which show you understand place value.

Give me an example to show that…
- multiplication can be thought of as repeated addition.
- division can be thought of as repeated subtraction.

Techniques

Show me how to… Tell me how to… Tell someone how to…
- add 37 and 85.
- subtract 29 from 53.
- calculate the perimeter of a polygon.
- construct a square using only a right-angled piece of card.
- construct two numbers with a given number as their highest common factor (their lowest common multiple).
- construct a number with an odd number of factors.
- find the area of a compound shape when two or more rectangles are put together.
- I think of a number, multiply by 3 and add 4; the answer is 13. What is the number?

Make up three examples which show that you know how to solve this type of problem.
- Calculate the missing angle when given two angles in a triangle.

Write a question/problem on… for the whole class to solve.
- symmetry.
- averages.

EXEMPLIFYING, SPECIALISING

Conjectures and Problems

What do you notice?
- $1 + 5 = 6$, $7 + 3 = 10$ ...

Do you think it will always happen?
- Odd + odd = even?

What if you try a bigger (smaller, simpler, more complex, harder) example?

Tell me what your current conjecture/reasoning/thinking/idea is.

What do you think the problem is asking?
- when it says 'without measuring the diagram'?
- Give an example of a story which illustrates $3 \times 5 = 15$
- Make up a word problem to which the answer is 50

Representations and Notation

Show me a way to....
- write fractions
- record on the label of this jar how many beans there are in it.
- use this equipment to show how you add 3 to 4.
- write down in figures the biggest number you can say in words.
- find 8/7 on a number line.
- demonstrate 4/5 with a rectangle.
- find 2/3 of 3/4 of something using a diagram.
- depict some given data with a line-graph.
- Tell me a story which would be represented by

- Find and compare different notations which are used to indicate division.

Explanations, Justifications, Reasoning

How would you explain (justify)....
- why the angles of a triangle add up to 180 degrees using paper and scissors?
- why half of a half is less than a half?
- why a half of a quarter is the same as a quarter of a half?
- why the area of a rectangle divided by the length of one side gives the length of the other side?
- why coordinates are useful for locating points?

Links, Relationships, Connections

Give an example of a relationship between...
- rectangles and cuboids
- adding and subtracting
- multiplying and dividing.

What is the same and what is different about....?
- subtracting and dividing
- fractions and decimals
- distances between points on a square grid using the grid lines, and ordinary distances
- 2 cm and 20 mm
- a 2 cm by 6 cm rectangle and a 3 cm by 4 cm rectangle?

EXEMPLIFYING, SPECIALISING

Primary Questions & Prompts — 17

Definitions

To be a... which aspects must be added?

- a week, what must be added to: Monday, Tuesday, Wednesday?
- a trapezium, what must be added to: opposite sides are parallel?

Tell me what is wrong with this:

- I am going to weigh the length of this brick
- Adding a number makes the answer bigger
- Multiplying by a number makes the answer bigger
- The denominator of a fraction is always bigger than the numerator
- A hexagon always has six equal sides
- A percentage can never be more than 100

To be a rectangle, which statements can be deleted?

- four right angles?
- (at least) three right angles?
- (at least) two right angles?
- (at least) one pair of parallel sides?
- two pairs of parallel sides?
- (at least) one pair of opposite sides equal?
- two pairs of opposite sides equal?
- diagonals bisect?
- sum of the interior angles is 360°?

Facts, Theorems and Properties

Complete, and delete or correct properties as required:

In a triangle:
- sum of the internal angles is 180°
- two edges are equal
- one edge is greater than the sum of the other two edges
- one angle is more than 90°
- at most one angle is more than 90°
- there are three edges and three angles
- no two of the edges are equal in length
- two edges are equal in length and all three angles are different
- two angles are equal but all three edges are different in length
- no angle is 0°

A decimal has:
- an infinite number of decimal places
- a decimal point
- a digit in every place
- zeros at the front
- zeros at the end

To make a... become a... complete the list of properties:

- quadrilateral become a parallelogram

Examples and Counter-examples

What (additional) properties must a... have so that it is an example of a...?

- a triple of numbers to be an example of three numbers which could be the lengths of the edges of a triangle?
- a rectangle to be also a square?
- a rhombus to be also a square?

How can you change... in order to turn it into an example of...?

- the question $5 - 4 = ?$ so that the answer is negative?
- $3 + 4 = 7$ into a subtraction?
- $3 \times 4 = 12$ into a division?
- a quadrilateral with equal sides into a square

What (additional) properties must... have so that it is a counter-example to the conjecture that...?

- two positive numbers
  and
  multiplication makes bigger?
- a number which is divisible by 3
  and
  is also divisible by 6?

What do you have to do to... in order to turn it into a counter example to the conjecture that...?

- $5 - 4 = 1$
  and
  subtraction makes smaller?

Techniques

Complete the solution:

The following is what Jane did to solve this problem "How much of a pizza can each person have if they are going to share equally, when 3 people have £2.40 each and 5 people have £3.30 each, and a pizza costs £4.60?":
$3 \times 2.40 + 5 \times 3.30 = 23.70$ *complete the solution.*

Complete these statements:

$7 + \triangle = 3 + \blacksquare$

$(6 + \triangle) \times \blacksquare = 100$

Complete this tables square:

×	3	?	?	7
?	6	?	?	?
?	?	?	25	?
?	?	?	?	56

Delete the unnecessary steps:

When doing the subtraction: $11 - 7$;
count up to 7;
count up to 11;
count from 7 to 11.

Correct this child's homework:

COMPLETING, DELETING, CORRECTING

Conjectures and Problems

What other information is needed in order to answer this question?

- John has 3 pencils. How many pencils do John and Mary have together?
- Two numbers differ by 4. What is their product?
- On a clock face the hour hand is between 3 and 4. What is the time?
- On a clock face the minute hand is on 6. What is the time?
- In a class the red group has an average mark of 6 out of 10, and the blue group has an average mark of 5 out of 10; what was the class average?

Delete information in order to create a problem.

- At one supermarket, butter costs 65 pence per pack. This is two pence less per pack than butter at another shop. If you need to buy 4 packs of butter, how much more will you pay at the second shop?

What additional information do you need…

- to determine which one of the shapes on this poster (in this box, on this desk, etc.) I am thinking of.
- to find the age of a shepherd given that he has five goats and three sheep?

Representations and Notation

Complete the missing parts in the following representations so that the information presented is the same in both modes:

- Complete the missing parts in the bar chart and table

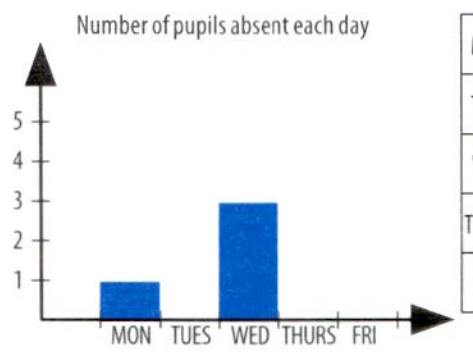

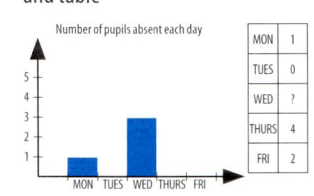

  Number of pupils absent each day

MON	1
TUES	0
WED	?
THURS	4
FRI	2

- Complete the missing parts in

  $$\frac{42}{} = \frac{}{30} = 3.5$$

- Complete the missing part in 'The perimeter of a square is 20 cm. The area is … .'

Correct the notation in:

- $100 + 1 = 1001$
- $3 \times 7 = 21 + 5 = 26$
- Area $= 2 \text{ cm} \times 3 \text{ cm} = 6 \text{ cm}$
- Perimeter of a 5 cm square is 25 cm^2

Explanations, Justifications, Reasoning

Correct the following argument:

- The length of this line is 7 cm

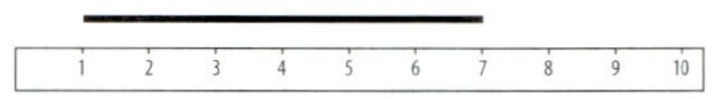

  1 2 3 4 5 6 7 8 9 10

- Delete any angle which can be derived from others

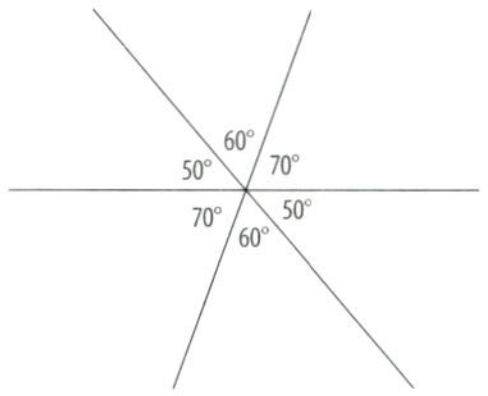

  (angles shown: 50°, 60°, 70°, 70°, 60°, 50°)

If … then … because … .

- If you start at one and count up in threes then you cannot get to 12 because … .
- If angle a is acute then angle b is … because … .

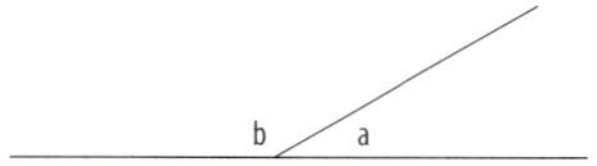

  (diagram showing angles b and a on a line)

Links, Relationships, Connections

… and … are the same in that both are … but different in that … .

- Fractions and decimals are the same in that both are … , but different in that … .
- 'If you add two numbers the answer is 10.' 'If you double two numbers and then add them the answer is 20.' These statements are the same because … but different because … .
- On a number line, going forward four steps and then back two steps, or going back two steps and then forward four steps are the same in that … , but different in that … .

What needs to be corrected so that

- 0.333 is equivalent to 1/3?
- this graph represents someone's pulse rate while exercising?

COMPLETING, DELETING, CORRECTING

Primary Questions & Prompts

19

Definitions

What is the same and what different about these definitions of a pattern?

- A sequence of shapes that repeats, e.g. ○▲■○▲■○▲■..., and a sequence of numbers 1, 3, 6, 11, 13, 16, 21, 23, 26...

What is the same and what is different about these definitions of negative numbers?

- A positive number with a minus sign in front
- A number less than zero
- What you get when you take a bigger number from a smaller number

Sort the following definitions into an order which reflects their interdependency:

- rectangle, parallelogram, square

Is… really a…

- is a parallelogram with a right angle really a rectangle?

Facts and Properties

What is the same and what different about…

- sides of a triangle, wheels on a tricycle, corners on a pirate's hat?
- this shape on the desk and this one in the feely bag?
- the 1 and the 3 in 13?

Sort the following according to…

- whether they roll or don't roll
- their size: numbers
- their symmetry properties: square, rectangle, rhombus, kite etc.
- their angle properties: square, rectangle, rhombus, kite etc.

Is… a property of…

- is 'equal sides' really a property of rectangles?

Examples and Counterexamples

What is the same and what is different about…

- two close numbers on the hundred square?
- multiples of 3 and 6?
- doubling/halving odd and even numbers?
- square numbers and numbers that are not square?
- a number whose square is 4 and a number whose square is 3?

Sort the following according to…

- whether they are multiples of 2 or multiples of 5 or both (using a Venn diagram)

Is… an example of…

- is 4/9 an example of a recurring decimal?
- is zero a number?

Techniques

What is the same and what is different about…

- counting objects in 1s and in 2s?
- counting money in 1p coins and 10p coins?
- the number of objects in the jar and the symbol on the lid?
- long multiplication by the grid method and traditional long multiplication?

Sort the following according to…

- the accuracy of your results when you measure the length of the classroom using: tape measure, length of foot, strides, metre stick.

Put in order…

- children according to how many counters they each have
- some instructions for converting decimals to fractions

Is… a technique for…

- is counting on using a number line a technique for subtraction?
- is multiplication a technique for making things bigger?

COMPARING, SORTING, ORGANISING

Conjectures and Problems

What is the same and what is different about…?

- a number with one digit and a number with two digits
- where you would place 10 on a counting stick imagined as 0 to 20 and on a counting stick imagined as 0 to 100
- multiples of 2 and multiples of 10

Sort these problems according to…

- the size of the answer:
  e.g. $2 + 3$, $1 + 1$, $5 - 2$, …
- the approximate size of the answers: e.g.
  50×2.5, 2.6×50, 5×2.5, 5×25, 260×5

Is… really a…?

- is 'how many tennis balls will fill this bucket?' really a problem which can be solved using a calculation?
- is 'a hundred squares need 310 matches' really an appropriate conjecture for

  ▢▢▢ …

Representations and Notation

What is the same and what is different about…?

- a triangle and a square
- $3 + 4 = 7$ and $4 + 3 = 7$ and $7 = 3 + 4$
- $3 + 2$ and $4 + 1$

Put these in order…

- put the following into an order which makes it easy to convert from one to the next: fractions, percentages, decimals

Is… a useful notation for…?

- is a number line a useful representation for a fraction?
- is a number line a useful representation for money?

Explanations, Justifications, Reasoning

What is the same and what is different about…?

- "3, 6, 9, 12, 15 …",
  "the next number is 18" and
  "the sequence goes up in 3s"

Is… a good explanation of…?

- having three sides a good explanation of a triangle?
- add a zero a good explanation of multiplying by 10?
- move the digits three places to the left a good explanation for multiplying 1.3 by 1000?

Is… a full explanation of…?

Which of these give a full explanation of what an even number is:
- two even numbers add to make an even number;
- if I divide an even number by two there is no remainder.

Links, Relationships, Connections

What is the same and what is different about…?

- one and 1?
- 3 and 4? 13 and 3? 10 and 100?
- a cone and a cylinder?
- these pictures?
- the 10s digits in the columns and the 10s digits in the rows of a 100 square?
- 1/2, 0.5, 50%, 4:8, 3/6, 1:2?

What is the connection between…?

- ten 1p coins and one 10p coin?
- the number of sides of a regular polygon and the size of the interior angle?

COMPARING, SORTING, ORGANISING

Definitions

Change… so that it describes a…

- the definition of a square so that it describes a rectangle.
- the description of a decimal so it describes a percentage.
- The even numbers start at zero and go up in twos. Change this so that it describes odd numbers.

Reverse the property to make a definition; is it then the same object?

- A single digit integer is less than 10.
- The sum of 3 consecutive numbers is divisible by 3.
- To say 'one more than' you say the next counting number.
- The diagonals of a parallelogram bisect each other.
- A square number is the sum of two consecutive triangular numbers.

Facts, Theorems and Properties

What do you get if you change… to…

- What do you get if you change one more than to one less than?
- What do you get if you give a triangle an extra side?
- What happens if you straighten part of a circle?
- What area do you get if you change a given rectangle to a different rectangle keeping the same perimeter?
- What happens to the area and perimeter of a shape if you make the sides three times longer?
- What do you get if you change 3.7 x 10 to 3.7 x 100 or 3.7 x 0.1?

Examples and Counter-examples

Change one aspect of the example so that…

- the numbers without changing the fact that the mean of 1,2,3,4,5 is 3
- an isoseles triangle so that it has 3 lines of symmetry.

Give me an example…

- where it would not be a good idea to measure length in millimetres.
- where it is not a good idea to display the data in a line graph.
- of a non-standard unit you might use to measure the capacity of a bucket.
- of a non-standard unit you might use to measure the mass of your teacher.
- of what the starting and finishing times might be if a journey takes half an hour.
- where multiplying by 10 does not put a zero on the end.

Techniques and instructions

Do this in at least… ways

- Describe at least two ways of adding 28 + 28, 3 + 4, 7 + 8.
- Multiply 23 by 19 in at least two ways.
- Describe the average of some data in at least two ways.
- Find the area of a rectangle in two ways.

Find out if this method works if …

- Find out if you can measure lengths with a ruler if the line is on the desk, the line is on a ball, the line is on the ceiling.
- Find out if you can find the area of a quadrilateral using length x width if it is not a rectangle.
- Find out if you can calculate percentages if the percentage is over 100.

CHANGING, VARYING, REVERSING, ALTERING

Conjectures and Problems

How would your conjecture change if you changed... to... ?

- Given a coil of string for which the estimated length is 50 cm, how would the conjecture change if it were straightened out?

Create a new problem by changing... to...

- a 30° angle in a right-angled triangle to 60°
- a 90° angle to a 92° angle
- A rectangle has four right angles. How many right angles can a pentagon have?

Representations and Notation

Demonstrate, write, show... using...

- the same subtraction (done with cubes) using the number line
- this data on a barchart, graph.
- one third of 9 using a picture.
- one third of 8 using a picture
- the mean average of two numbers in a picture
- Write 2km in m
- Write 2kg in g
- Write 2 minutes in seconds
- Write 2000 hours in fortnights

The calculation $(2 + 3) \times (1 + 5)$ can be solved as follows

×	2	3	
1	2	3	5
5	10	15	25
	12	18	30

Do the same for other numbers.

Explanations, Justifications, Reasoning

Explain, justify...

- Having explained why change from £1 when buying an object for 74p is 26p, explain your calculation if we know the change is 26p but we do not know the price of the object
- You make an estimate for the capacity of a jar using Centicubes. How would your estimate change if you were to use Multilink?
- You estimate the height of a door using the length of A4 paper as a non-standard unit. How would your estimate change if you were to use the width of the paper?
- Why does a Y1 teacher always give the children an even number to halve?
- On an analogue clock if the little hand is nearer to the 3 than the 4 what time might it be?
- Explain why this parallelogram does not have line symmetry.

- Change the shading on a shape so that it does not have line symmetry.

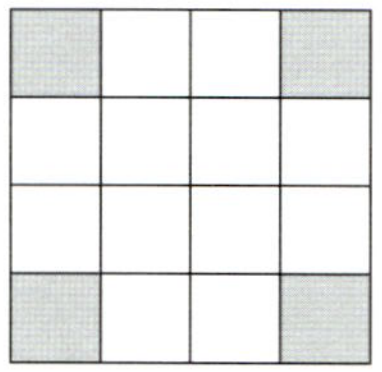

Links, Relationships, Connections

What if ...?

- If $3 + 4 = 7$, what else do I know?
- If $10 = 5 \times 2$, what else do I know?
- If we have a table of values we can draw a graph. If we have a graph can we construct a table of values?
- If we eat 8 blocks of a chocolate bar with 24 blocks we have eaten 1/3 of the bar. If we can see from the shape of the package that we have eaten 1/3 of the bar, can we say how many blocks have been eaten?
- From a sequence of pictures such as:

we can obtain a table and detect a pattern of adding on 3's. Can we go directly from the pictures to the formula? Conversely, can we go from the formula to the pictures?

- Find out if the area of a right-angled triangle is connected to the area of a rectangle

CHANGING VARYING REVERSING ALTERING

Definitions

Describe… in one word, one sentence, one expression, one diagram.
- with one word all quadrilaterals that have two pairs of parallel sides.
- with one word all quadrilaterals that have one pair of opposite sides parallel.
- in one sentence a square.
- in one sentence a litre.

Is it true that we can define… as… ?
- a 2D shape as one that we can draw?
- angle as a turn?
- a prime number as a number that has only 1 and itself as factors?
- a diagonal as a line that joins two corners/vertices of a polygon?

Facts and Properties

Of what is this an example?
- the angles in an equilateral triangle are equal.
- even numbers are multiples of 2.

Is it always, sometimes, never, true that… ?
- the diagonals of a quadrilateral bisect each other?
- two negatives make a positive?
- the angles of a triangle add up to 180°?
- all multiples of 3 have a digital root of 3, 6 or 9?

Describe… in one word, one sentence, one expression, one diagram.
- objects that roll
- two different ways of deciding if two things are equal

Examples and Counter-Examples

Of what is… an example or counter-example?
- 18, 6, 30, 60, 24
- 50, 20, 80, 70, 130

Is it always, sometimes, never, true that… ?
- a triangle has three sides?
- a quadrilateral has four right angles?
- length is best measured in metres?
- a bar chart is a clear way of displaying data?
- a prime number is odd?
- if you know the rule you can find any number in the sequence?

Techniques

Of what is… an example?
- 3/4 = 15/20

Is it always, sometimes, never, true that… ?
- multiplication makes bigger?
- if you see part of a shape you know what the whole shape is?

What can change, and what must still stay the same?
- The mean of 3, 5, and 7 is 5. What can be changed and yet the mean remains 5?
- To divide by 4, I can divide by two and then divide by two again. What can change and what must stay the same to divide by 6?
- How can the data in a pie chart be changed so that the pie chart still looks the same?
- How can brackets change the value of $27 - 3 \times 6 - 5$?

What happens in general… ?
- if I halve an odd number?
- if I halve a decimal number?
- to test for divisibility by 3?
- to test for divisibility by 4?

GENERALISING, CONJECTURING

Primary Questions & Prompts

Conjectures and Problems

Generalise:
- Given the average of three numbers, and a fourth, find the average of all four

Is it always, sometimes, never, true that . . . ?
- a 3D shape can roll if it has a curved surface?
- given a rectangle, you can always find another with the same area but larger perimeter?
- the sum of four consecutive numbers is divisible by four?

What can change, and what must still stay the same?
- to get another whole number answer to a problem similar to 'share £1000 between three people in the ratio 1:2:2'
- so that the probability of getting a red marble out of a bag is 1/2?

Representations and Notation

Of what is . . . an example?
- a cuboid an example?
- an equilateral triangle a particular case?

Is it always, sometimes, never, true that . . . ?
- the pictures on a pictogram represent one piece of data?
- all the boxes on a Carroll diagram have to be filled in?
- if the answer is in cm² it is an area?

What can change, and what must still stay the same?
- (2,3), (2,6) and (2,8) all lie on a straight line. What can change and what must stay the same for other points to lie on this line?

Explanations, Justifications, Reasoning

Of what is this a special case?
- square

What can change, and what must still stay the same?
- The answer is 24. What is the question?

Describe all . . . in one word, one sentence, one expression, one diagram.
- Describe why the sum of two odd numbers is always even.

Links, Relationships, Connections

Of what is this an example?
- 36 (e.g. square number, triangle number)

Is it always, sometimes, never, true that . . . ?
- between any two decimals there is another decimal?

What can change, and what must still stay the same....?
- in a method for converting a fraction to a decimal?

Describe in one word, one sentence, one expression, one diagram ...
- all numbers with this property (e.g. one more than a multiple of 7).
- the relationship between decimals and percentages
- the relationship between multiplying numbers and areas of rectangles

GENERALISING, CONJECTURING

Definitions

Is there anything else which is not an … which is described by this?

- Are there any fractions which are not less than one?
- Are there any primes that are not odd?
- Are there any even numbers which are not less than 20?
- Are there any numbers which are not less than 100? … 1000?
- Are there any four sided shapes that are not rectangles?
- Are there any circles which do not have curved edges?
- Are there any triangles which do not have three straight sides?

Why do we need to say … in the definition?

- What properties of a triangle do we need to state to be sure our shape is a triangle?
- What properties of a square do we need to state to be sure our shape is a square?
- What additional property would a rhombus need to make it a square?
- What additional property would a rectangle need to make it a square?

Facts, Theorems and Properties

How can we be sure that … ?

- 8 is an even number?
- an equilateral triangle is symmetrical?
- the sum of three consecutive numbers is divisible by 3?

Is it ever false that … ?

- adding one more to a number makes it bigger?
- a triangle has three sides?
- a regular polygon is also symmetrical?
- a polygon with all sides equal must have all angles equal?
- division makes numbers smaller?
- putting zero on the end of a number multiplies it by ten?
- adding tops and bottoms of two fractions gives their sum?

Examples and Counter-examples

Why is … an example of … ?

- $3 + 4 = 7$ an example of an addition sum?
- 6 an example of an even number?
- a square an example of a rectangle?
- 21:00 a way to write 9 o'clock?
- 5 mm an example of a metric length?
- Why is changing 1.275m to 1.3m an example of appropriate rounding when measuring the length of a desk?

Tell me what is wrong with …

- $3 - 7 = 4$.
- $1/2 + 1/2 = 2/4$.
- $1/3 + 1/3 = 2/6$.
- a triangle with four lines of symmetry.
- When the product of two numbers is 0, one or other of them must be 0, so if the product of two numbers is 1, one or other of them must be 1.

Techniques and Instructions

How can we be sure that … ?

- one more than four is five?
- this number is even?
- this shape is a square?
- this line is 1 metre long?
- $299 + 3 = 302$?
- we have all the possible ways of scoring 7 when rolling 2 dice?
- we have found all the prime factors of a given number?
- a point with certain given co-ordinates lies in the fourth quadrant?

Is it always true that … ?

- the sand-timer will run for one minute?
- subtraction always reverses the effect of addition?
- turning left and then turning right means you are facing the same direction as you were to start with?
- the median gives a useful measure of the average of a collection of numbers?
- John uses a standard written method, Amy uses a mental method. Is it true that Amy finishes first?

EXPLAINING, JUSTIFYING, VERIFYING, REFUTING

Conjectures and Problems

What does the problem want?
What problem are we trying to solve?
What is your conjecture?
What do you want to find, show, prove?
Write down your thoughts with the evidence that you have.

- Daffy the duck has fewer than 10 eggs. She counts them in twos and there is one left over. She counts them in threes and there is one left over. How many eggs does she have?

- John makes six large iced sponge cakes for the school fete. Each cake is 3cm thick. He pays £6.08 for the ingredients. He cuts each cake into 8 rows and 6 columns. He puts the pieces of cake into boxes with 15 pieces in each. He eats any left over pieces. Each full box weighs 480g. He sells all the boxes for £2.50 each. What profit does he make on each box?

What does... (some term)... mean?
- parallel?
- = ?
- + ?

Explain the role of... in this problem.
- subtraction in this problem: 9 is the output from an 'Add 2' function machine, what was the input?
- inverse operation in this problem: 45 is the output from a 'Multiply by 5' function machine, what was the input?
- distance in this problem: it takes me 45 mins at 60 km/h to go from A to B, and I come back at 40 km/h. How long was I travelling?

Representations and Notation

**Verify that... means the same as....
Why is... the same as...?**
- this barchart captures everything from the data.
- $3 + 4 = 4 + 3$.

Explanations, Justifications, Reasoning

How can we be sure that this explanation works in all cases?
- adding one to a counting number gives the next counting number.
- adding one to an integer gives the next integer.
- using 10p and 1p coins we can explain place value for all numbers less than 100.
- moving the digits of a number one place to the left will multiply that number by 10.

How is/are... used in...?
- doubles used in finding near doubles?
- halving used in dividing by four?
- rulers used in measurement?
- analogue clocks used to measure time?
- the angle sum of a triangle used to find an unknown angle in a triangle?

Explain or refute why...
- two identical right angled scalene triangles can be put together to make an isosceles triangle, a kite, a rectangle, a parallelogram.
- if 3 is more than 2 and 4 is more than 3 then 4 is more than 2.
- it is appropriate to use a line-graph to display specified data.

Explain what is inadequate about saying that...
- 2 o'clock always follows after 1 o'clock.
- a shape which has four equal sides is a square.
- rotate this shape through 90°.
- a shape with three lines of symmetry is an equilateral triangle.

Links, Relationships, Corrections

Explain connections between... and...
- 7×8 and 70×80.
- division and multiplication.
- decimals and fractions.
- greatest common divisor of two numbers and their lowest common multiple.

Why do..., ..., & ... all give the same answer?
- $21 - 17$,
  $41 - 37$
  and
  $101 - 97$.
- 6×8,
  2×24,
  and
  3×16.
- rotate 90° clockwise about A
  and
  rotate 270° anticlockwise about A.

EXPLAINING, JUSTIFYING, VERIFYING, REFUTING

7 - DYRSZLAG'S ORIGINAL LIST

The work in this booklet was stimulated initially by a list of techniques made by Zygfryd Dyrszlag [1984] and translated from Polish into English for us by Anna Sierpinska. Dyrszlag worked under the supervision of Zofia Krygowska who believed that '... analogy, schematising, defining, deduction and reduction, coding and algorithmising may and should be developed in children's mathematical activity from the very beginning of mathematics teaching' [Krygowska 1984].

Dyrszlag saw mathematical understanding as occurring in two ways: descriptive understanding, which related to static meanings such as definitions, and operative understanding, which referred to meanings revealed through dynamic mathematical processes [Sierpinska, p118].

Effectively we have separated Dyrszlag's static and dynamic 'understandings' of mathematics and used them to create a two-dimensional grid, in which processes can be made to act on various kinds of mathematical statement, providing many opportunities to develop higher-order mathematical thinking.

8 - BACKGROUND

In this final section, we offer some observations about the role of questioning in teaching, and point to some theoretical justifications for its importance. We look at questioning as a social activity enculturating pupils into practices which extend beyond the classroom. Then we consider different kinds of questions related to their purposes. We consider then meta-questioning, that is, drawing attention to the types of questions we are asking pupils, as a pedagogical device in itself. Whatever style of teaching you use, paying attention to the structure, form and implicit messages in your questions is worthwhile.

Questioning as Social and Psychological Activity

A learner's experience in the classroom frames the view she will have about the subject. If she is asked closed questions with attention only to right answers, then getting an answer, any answer, will become the aim of mathematics; if all that is asked is that work is neat and tidy, then neatness and completion will become the aims of mathematics; if she is asked to express her thoughts about a concept, then expressing her own thoughts will become the aim; if she is asked to think, to develop relationships and structures, to compare them to, and eventually express them in, conventional forms, then these will become the aims of mathematics. The questions and prompts used, and the responses to these which are accepted, become the model of mathematical behaviour for the learner.

It follows that if pupils are embedded in a context in which a rich variety of question types are being used, they are likely to pick up a sense of the subject as a richly embroidered fabric.

Questioning in Different Ways

Teachers' questions and prompts play a major role in the teaching and learning of mathematics. So, of course, do textbook questions. Whatever the source of questions they are often rather limited in style. Janet Ainley studied forms of questions [Ainley 1987] and came up with a list [Ainley 1988] of four main types:

- pseudo-questions such as "We don't do that in mathematics, now, do we?" at most seek compliance to establish a practice;
- genuine questions in which the teacher seeks information because they do not know the answer;
- testing questions for which the teacher knows the answer, and the pupil knows this;
- directing questions to provoke a pupil to think further.

How do we recognise which type of question we are asking? You might think that you always know before you ask, but a little observation will reveal that often it is when you are suddenly surprised by a response that you realise that you already had in mind what would be an acceptable answer. In such moments it may be possible to catch yourself before you alter the question in order to 'get the answer you want', a process described beautifully by John Holt [1964], and by Heinrich Bauersfeld [1994] who uses the term funnelling, and in the folklore as playing the game 'Guess what is in my mind'.

As soon as you catch yourself funnelling, or playing the game, you have a choice: to carry on or to bail out. Paying attention to your own questioning can help sensitise you to moments when you are about to embark on funnelling, so offering a moment of choice as to whether to go that route.

Ainley goes further and identifies three subcategories of directing: checking questions to explore certainty; opening questions to encourage exploration; and structuring questions to help pupils organise their thinking.

Questions in these three subcategories can all stimulate mathematical thinking and learning and in practice teachers develop their own collection of devices. However, in our experience, many questions intended to encourage thinking are obscure and difficult to answer. They are either too general, or they rely on sophisticated articulation of mental processes. Questions such as "why...?" and "how did you work that out?" are often answered with blank looks or vague comments like "I just did it, it's obvious". Questions which are derived from ways of thinking about mathematics, such as those offered here, are likely to be useful because they reflect mathematical thinking.

Questioning Ourselves

Most adults seem naturally to ask 'teacherly' or 'testing' type questions of children. They get this from having been children themselves, and having been enculturated into those kinds of questions. Children very quickly discover the power of asking questions, and for a time they exploit it ruthlessly! They soon recognise 'teacherly' testing-type questions, and can mimic this behaviour in their play.

The questions which enriched our own learning become our repertoire. They come from our own teachers, from our mentors and tutors, from colleagues, and sometimes they arise spontaneously without an obvious source. Since as teachers we are tempted to tread the same paths repeatedly, our pupils get to know what kinds of questions we use. If we continue to use stylised questions our pupils will stop paying attention and will develop a restricted impression of the practices of mathematics. On the other hand if every question is different, pupils will be unlikely to notice any pattern or structure in our questions, and may even become frustrated and confused. They are unlikely to internalise those questions or to get any lasting impression of mathematical thinking.

When we get an unexpected response from a pupil there is a moment of opportunity to note what question we asked and what the situation is, so that we can try to reproduce that later. Relying on questions in published textbooks or lesson scripts we may never develop our questioning at all, because the questioning has to be generated from inside, as part of our perspective, our view of mathematics and of learning mathematics.

One powerful way to learn to ask 'good' questions is to give rein to your own curiosity. Approaching the task of teaching by being genuinely interested in what pupils are thinking enables you to ask questions about the mathematics, or about the pupils, or about the pupils' ways and methods of learning mathematics, in a way which is difficult if your interest is only in the answers.

Even test situations and technical performance of limited skills can be questioned. A prompt which requires thought about a routine can reveal more about competence and understanding than mere performance of the routine. For instance "tell me three numbers which would be 3.50 if they were rounded to two decimal places" is non-routine, revealing, and provokes thought and rule-use.

Becoming a good questioner is not a matter of using someone else's list of questions (even our list!), but of developing questioning as a personal activity with mathematics. Asking oneself "what can I ask of my pupils?" rather than "How can I get them to say what I am seeing?" passes responsibility and initiative to learners.

Questioning Questioning

A few question types can be used over and over until the moment comes when you suddenly ask "What question am I going to ask you?". Usually the first time you ask this, the pupils are thrown; they have no idea what you mean. So you point out that you usually ask a question of the type … (e.g. 'can you give me an example', or 'what does this term mean?' or 'what is your range of choices?'). Then you ask your usual question and carry on. After a period of time in which you occasionally repeat your 'meta-question', the pupils start to recognise the kinds of question you are asking. Then you can begin to fade your use of that type of question and introduce others. That does not mean that the first form is no longer needed, but rather that you are expecting them to ask themselves that kind of question. This process of being repetitive, then provoking pupils to recognise the type of question, then reducing your use while expecting them to take over, is often referred to as scaffolding and fading.

The term scaffolding was introduced by Wood, Bruner & Ross [1976] in the context of problem solving, to describe situations in which a relative expert temporarily controls elements of the task that are initially beyond the learner's capacity. Without the concomitant notion of fading, so that pupils' enquiry can take over from teachers' direction, scaffolding fails to have the desired effect. Unless the teacher reduces the directness of their interventions, pupils are likely to remain dependent on the teacher asking certain questions. They are thus only being trained in dependency. Instead of scaffolding as a temporary measure, the teacher is built in as part of the foundations.

At first the teacher asks direct questions of a particular type; later they offer increasingly less direct prompts to the same question, until the pupils are using that question themselves more or less spontaneously. If the teacher begins to reduce the density of their interventions of one particular type (say a particular kind of question), pupils' attention can be directed to it, and they can begin to become less dependent on the teacher in that respect. Thus all uses of a given question type can be placed somewhere on a spectrum from directed to prompted to spontaneous.

Our questions used repetitively or randomly are likely to be no more effective than any other questions. Our questions can however provide a source for development of pupils' own use of questions to help them learn through the teacher's repeated use followed by gradual fading of explicit use.

Questioning for Learning Mathematics

There is another way questions such as ours scaffold. Because they relate directly to the structures of pure mathematics they influence the learner's own construction of mathematical understanding, not just in terms of how they pose inner questions, but also in their perceptions and attitudes, and in their knowledge.

For example, asking pupils to find special cases of quadrilaterals suggests that looking for special cases is a useful thing to do, and also aids their learning about shapes; asking pupils to construct their own examples of, say, large or long decimal numbers suggests that exemplifying is a useful thing to do when doing mathematics, as well as helping them learn about the structures and characteristics of number names and decimal notation.

It is important to see that these developments take place within a social situation of talk, discussion, questions, prompts and answers, in which the teacher and other pupils are as much a part of what mathematical activity is as what is in a textbook, on the flashcards, or on the board. In fact, what is said mathematically in relation to these artefacts is more important than what is written on them because of the social nature of the classroom.

In this social situation the learner is experiencing a range of activities, challenges, responses, rewards and disappointments in the course of the work. Each of these contributes in some way to her constructed understandings. Our main excitement about Dyrszlag's approach was that his questions offered so many opportunities for the active learner to relate her knowledge to new ideas, borderline examples, contradictions, different representations, existing knowledge, and new experiences. In other words, they provide devices through which the teacher, who is aware that learners build their own understandings anyway, can work through, rather than against, this recognition.

Questioning Understanding

What does it mean to understand a concept such as fraction, angle, algorithm, or semi-circle? Many authors have written at length, and developed vocabularies of technical terms in order to emphasise distinctions of importance to them. For example, Skemp [1969] distinguished between instrumental and relational understanding. Instrumental understanding means being able to carry out routine techniques, often memorised or automated without a sense of why it works. Relational understanding refers to having sufficient sense of what the technique does, and why, to be able to modify it or augment it or otherwise deal with unusual situations. Gattegno [1987] made roughly the same distinction when he proposed that 'only awareness is educable', which is complemented by 'only behaviour is trainable', and 'only emotion is harnessable' [Mason 1994].

We have found that asking learners to construct their own mathematical objects to meet specified constraints reveals the scope and breadth of their appreciation and understanding of concepts in a way which is not accessed through setting traditional exercises (Watson & Mason 2004). Furthermore, engaging in such construction tasks often extends and deepens learners' appreciation. They become aware of aspects which can be varied or generalised which they had not previously appreciated. The same applies to routine examination-type tasks: by constructing their own variations and comparing with what others produce, learners become aware of the range of questions which form a class of 'similar problems', thus preparing them to respond more flexibly under examination conditions.

Some people argue that we only ever learn to do things in a particular context. This theory is useful for explaining why it is that people can display considerable routine skills in examinations but not be able to use the same techniques in a context outside of the classroom. The same theory can be used to explain why people can often perform techniques perfectly well outside of a classroom, but appear not to know what to do when asked to do the same thing in class. Learning is seen as situated in context. Movement between contexts is often problematic.

We are not ignoring these ideas, nor the importance of practical and everyday mathematics. We are starting from a different place, believing that all school children are culturally entitled to have a genuine introduction to what is agreed to be pure mathematics. We think that very bright pupils are usually identified as such because they do not seem to require explicit mention of mathematical processes or ways of thinking, but most pupils require explicit and implicit immersion in such practices in order to come to recognise and carry out those practices for themselves.

Questioning which Reflects Mathematical Structure

It turns out that when we look at our view of mathematical structure it is inescapably connected to a constructivist view of learning.

Vygotsky [Wertsch 1985] writes about how teachers, through interaction, can help learners function at a higher, more complex, mental level through displaying that functioning themselves, and carefully supporting the learner through those processes, helping them do today what they will be able to do for themselves tomorrow. The important point here is that the aim is to think in a more complex way; this is not necessarily always true of a teacher showing someone what to do and how to do it, doing it with them and then going away while they try another one. It will only be true if the teacher has consciously supported the learner through to a higher level of thinking.

When children first encounter something new they naturally see it in terms of what they already know. They may be aware of the whole but unaware of details. For example a new shape may be identified holistically. With repeated exposure children become aware of details. They begin to make distinctions (perhaps vertices and edges). To be aware of properties of the object which make it what it is, depends on distinguishing significant features. Awareness of properties make it possible to become aware of relationships between properties. Pierre and Dina van Hiele [Fuys et al.1984] turned this observation into a sequence of levels of geometric awareness:

- visualisation (holistic)
- descriptive analytic (distinction making)
- informal deduction (properties)
- formal deduction (relationships)
- rigour, meta-mathematical (structure)

which apply to mathematics education more generally [van Hiele 1986, Mason 1996]. Being aware of the hierarchical structure can suggest appropriate questions, neither too simplistic nor too sophisticated, to ask pupils as they make contact with a new idea.

One of the exciting things about mathematics is that an idea which is the result of hard complex thinking when it is first encountered can then become an element, part of the raw material, for further thought. For instance, an understanding of the naming of large numbers or the meaning of non-unitary fractions can be hard to achieve for a young learner without many experiences, practical demonstrations, discussions and so on. Finally the learner is able to relate the idea to a conventional notation and maybe relate some fractions to each other and even have a grasp of abstraction in being able to talk about the purpose of different parts of the notation. The learner has actually altered the structure of their attention by becoming aware not just of an idea, but of details and distinctions, properties and relationships. A few months later, large numbers and their naming becomes routine and unexceptional; a few years later, non-unitary fractions in conventional notation may be seen as starting points for working with rational expressions. The concept has been reified [Sfard, 1994] that is, has become an object, a thing in its own right to be further manipulated, developed, combined, generalised, abstracted and so on. Gray & Tall [1994] coined the term procept to refer to a process becoming a 'thing', while retaining both its action and its concept.

This is how learners learn anything: forming a view, becoming familiar with it, using it, adapting it and developing it to take account of new challenges, and exchanging ideas about it with others through language and other interactions so that what was initially hazy and ill-formed becomes an element used to express further hazy ideas built upon it.

Belief about Teaching

Transmissional styles of teaching, and styles dependent on performance, provide opportunities for development of thinking only to those few learners who are able to spot and use deeply implicit yet helpful forms of thought. They are able to make useful connections for themselves. Our questions, relating closely to mathematics and to how people learn, model the processes of learning and relating mathematics explicitly for all pupils.

A first reading of some of our examples may have suggested to you that we had in mind only the brightest pupils, those who 'need stretching', or to whom we might wish to present 'extensions', or our own children. On the contrary, we believe that questions such as ours enable all children to learn mathematics, not by making it easy, relevant, accessible or rote-learnt, but by helping them become better thinkers.

BIBLIOGRAPHY

Ainley, J. 1987, Telling Questions, Mathematics Teaching, 118, p24-26.

Ainley, J. 1988, Perceptions of Teachers' Questioning Styles, in Barbas, A. (Ed.)Proceedings of the 12th Conference of the International Group for the Psychology of Mathematics Education, Veszprem, Hungary, pp.92-99.

Bauersfeld, H. 1994, 'Theoretical Perspectives on Interaction in the Mathematics Classroom', in Biehler R. et al. (Eds) The Didactics of Mathematics as a Scientific Discipline, Kluwer, Dordrecht.

Dyrszlag, Z. 1984, Sposoby Kontroli Rozumienia Pojec Matematycznych, Oswiata i Wychowanie 9, B p42-43.

Gattegno, C. 1987, The Science of Education Part I: theoretical considerations, Educational Solutions, New York.

Holt, J. 1964 How Children Fail, Penguin, Harmondsworth.

Kieren, T. 1994, Bonuses of Understanding Mathematical Understanding, in Robitaille, D. Wheeler, D. & Kieran, C. (eds.) Selected Lectures from the 7th International Congress on Mathematical Education, Les Presses de l'Université Laval, Quebec p211-228.

Krygowska, Z. 1988, Composants De l'Activité Mathématique Qui Devaient Jouer Le Rôle Essentiel Dans La Mathématique Pour Tous, Educational Studies in Mathematics 19, p423-433.

Mason J. 1994, Professional Development and Practitioner Research, Chreods 7, p3-12.

Mason, J. 1996, Wholeness, Distinctions, and Actions in Mathematics Education, ME822 Reader Block IV, Open University, Milton Keynes p5-14.

Sierpinska, A. 1994, Understanding in Mathematics, Falmer Press, London.

Sfard, A. 1994, Reification as the Birth of Metaphor, For the Learning of Mathematics, 14 (1) p44-55.

Skemp, R. 1969, The Psychology of Mathematics, Penguin, Harmondsworth.

Fuys, D., Geddes, D. & Tischler, R. (Eds.) 1985, English Translation of Selected Writings of Dina van Hiele-Geldof and Pierre van Hiele, Brooklyn College School of Education, Brooklyn, ERIC document 289 697.

van Hiele, P. 1986, Structure and Insight: a theory of mathematics education, Academic Press, Orlando.

Watson, A. & Mason, J. 2004, Mathematics as a Constructive Activity: the role of learner-generated examples, Erlbaum, Mahwah.

Wertsch, J. 1985, Vygotsky and the Social Formation of Mind, Harvard University Press, Cambridge.

Wood, D. Bruner, J. & Ross, G. 1976, The Role of Tutoring in Problem Solving, J. Child Psychology, 17, p89-100.

GENERAL QUESTIONS AND PROMPTS

Exemplifying Specialising	Completing Deleting Correcting	Comparing Sorting Organising
Give me one or more examples of… Describe, Demonstrate, Tell, Show, Choose, Draw, Find, Locate, an example of… Is… an example of…? What makes… an example? Find a counter-example of…	What <u>must</u> be added, removed, altered, in order to allow, ensure, contradict,…? What <u>can</u> be added, removed, altered, without affecting …? Tell me what is wrong with …. What needs to be changed so that…?	What is the same and different about…? Sort or organise the following according to… Is it or is it not…?

Changing Varying Reversing Altering	Generalising Conjecturing	Explaining Justifying Verifying Refuting
What do you get if you change…? What if…? If this is the answer to a similar question, what was the question? Do… in two (or more) ways. What is quickest, easiest,…?	Of what is this an example? What happens in general? Is it always, sometimes, never …? Describe all possible… as succinctly as you can. What can change and what has to stay the same so that… is still true?	Explain why…, Give a reason… How can we be sure that…? Tell me what is wrong with… Is it always true that…? How is… used in…? Explain role or use of…

Extract from
Primary *Questions & Prompts*
Copyright © 2004 Association of Teachers of Mathematics

GENERAL QUESTIONS AND PROMPTS

	Exemplifying Specialising	Completing Deleting Correcting	Comparing Sorting Organising	Changing Varying Reversing Altering	Generalising Conjecturing	Explaining Justifying Verifying Refuting
Vocabulary and Definitions						
Facts, Theorems and Properties						
Examples and Counter-examples						
Techniques and Instructions						
Conjectures and Problems						
Representations and Notation						
Explanations Justifications Reasoning						
Links Relationships Connections						

Extract from
Primary *Questions & Prompts*
Copyright © 2004 Association of Teachers of Mathematics